NOW YOU CAN READ....
JESUS'S WONDERFUL MIRACLES

STORY RETOLD BY LEONARD MATTHEWS

ILLUSTRATION BY MARK BERGIN

Published by Rourke Publications, Inc., P.O. Box 3328, Vero Beach, Florida 32964. Copyright © 1984 by Rourke Publications, Inc. All copyrights reserved. No part of this book may be reproduced in any form without written permission from the publisher. Printed in the United States of America.

The Publishers acknowledge permission from Brimax Books for the use of the name "Now You Can Read" and "Large Type For First Readers" which identify Brimax Now You Can Read series.

Library of Congress Cataloging in Publication Data

Matthews, Leonard.
Jesus's wonderful miracles.

(Now you can read—Bible stories)
Summary: Retells the stories of the miracles performed by Jesus Christ, including the feeding of the five thousand and the marriage in Cana.
1. Jesus Christ—Miracles—Juvenile literature.
[1. Jesus Christ—Miracles. 2. Miracles. 3. Bible stories—N.T.] I. Title. II. Series.
BT366.M38 1984 226'.709505 84-8386
ISBN 0-86625-301-7

GROLIER ENTERPRISES CORP.

NOW YOU CAN READ. . . .
JESUS'S WONDERFUL MIRACLES

In His lifetime, Jesus worked
many miracles. His first miracle
took place at a wedding. He and
His mother had been invited to the
wedding of some friends. Several of
His followers went with Him.
Before the wedding was over,
all the wine had been drunk. This
made the newly married couple
unhappy. Mary, the mother of
Jesus, asked Him if He could help.
Jesus pointed to six large jars.

"Fill those with water," Jesus said. "Then pour some and drink it."
Everyone was surprised. The water had been changed to wine. It was a happy wedding after all!

Some time later, a rich man stopped Jesus in the street. "My son is very ill," the man cried. "Please come and see him before he dies." Jesus replied, "Return home. Your son will live." The man was so happy when he arrived home. His son was already better.

Another miracle Jesus performed was
in Bethesda. Bethesda had a pool. Its
water was thought to cure sick people.
Jesus saw a lame man there. "I
cannot reach the pool," said the
man sadly.

"Get up," said Jesus. "Pick up your bed and walk." The man had not walked for many years. Suddenly, he found he *could* walk. When the lame man turned to thank Jesus, Jesus had gone.

In those days, the land where Jesus lived was ruled by the city of Rome. The people who lived there did not like the Romans. One day a Roman officer called to Jesus.

"My faithful servant is dying,"
the officer told Jesus. "I believe
that only you can save him."
It was strange that a Roman officer
would ask anyone for help. Jesus
was pleased because the Roman
officer believed in Him.

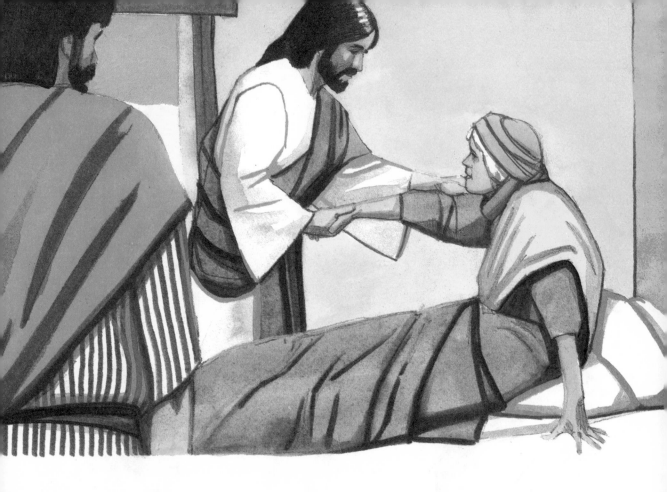

"You have faith in me," Jesus said. "Your servant will be healed." Even as He spoke, the servant back home sat up in bed. He was better.

Jesus then went to see the mother-in-law of His friend Peter. She had a bad fever.

As soon as Jesus touched her hand, Peter's mother-in-law rose from her bed. The fever had gone. A few days later Jesus was walking with His followers. A woman touched His robe. Jesus turned around. "I have been ill for twelve years," she said. "Please cure me." "You are cured because you trust in me," Jesus said. At once, the woman was well again.

Peter was a fisherman and a follower of Jesus. Once, he and his friends spent a night fishing. They caught nothing. Next morning, Jesus came by. "Put out your nets again," said Jesus. Suddenly their nets were so full of fish they could only just pull them in. Jesus had worked another miracle!

Jesus once cured ten men of leprosy. This illness could not be cured. As soon as they were cured, nine men went to tell the priests. The priests were the enemies of Jesus. Only one man stayed to thank Jesus.

At another time, a dead boy was carried past Jesus. His mother was crying. This made Jesus sad. "Arise!" He said quietly to the boy. The boy opened his eyes and came to life. His happy mother thanked Jesus over and over again.

One day Jesus came to the town of Bethsaida. There, He met a blind man. The man reached out his hands. Jesus touched him. "I can see! I see men. They look like trees," the man cried. Jesus touched the man again. "Now I can see everything clearly," said the man.

So Jesus went on His way, moving
from one city to another,
performing one miracle after
another. Soon everyone was
talking about Him and pointing
to Him as He passed. Sometimes He
would be invited into a house to
eat a meal and teach.

Once, He was in a house when a big crowd gathered outside. Suddenly, a man on a stretcher was lowered through a hole in the ceiling. The man could not walk and this was the only way his friends could get him into the house. Jesus touched him. "Arise," Jesus said. Everyone gasped when the man stood up.

The man who had been crippled thanked Jesus and walked home. It was yet another miracle.

Jesus had travelled far. He was very tired. He and His followers decided to cross the Sea of Galilee. There they could rest quietly. However, many people had followed them. Some were already waiting for them. Although Jesus was tired, He spoke for many hours. How kind He was.

Five thousand people listened to Him. They were all very hungry but they were far from town. What could they eat? They had only five loaves of bread and two fishes. Jesus took the loaves and fishes. He blessed them. Then, He broke them into small pieces.

"Now feed the people," Jesus said to His followers. Many times they came back for more food. At last all the five thousand people had been fed. Twelve baskets of food were left. It was amazing.

Jesus now wanted to pray alone. He told His followers to cross the sea and wait for him. No sooner had they set out than a great storm blew up. It seemed as though the boat would sink.

Jesus saw the danger. He walked across the water toward the boat. His followers were afraid. Was it a ghost? Jesus called out to them. Peter shouted: "If it is really you, help me to walk on the water, too."

"Then come," said Jesus. Peter got out of the boat. He started to sink. Jesus grasped him and walked him back to the boat. "You should have more faith in me," He smiled as the storm died away.

All these appear in the pages of the story. Can you find them?

Jesus

Mary, the mother
of Jesus

a fishing boat

the thankful leper

a Roman officer

basket of loaves

Now tell the story in your own words.